Over A Bridge!
A Kid's Guide To Budapest, Hungary

Photography By John D. Weigand
Poetry By Penelope Dyan

Bellissima Publishing, LLC
Jamul, California
www.bellissimapublishing.com

Copyright © 2013 by Penny D. Weigand & John D. Weigand

All rights reserved. No part of this book may be
reproduced or transmitted in any form or by any means,
electronic or mechanical, including photocopying,
recording, or by any other means, or by any information or
storage retrieval system, without permission from the publisher.

ISBN 978-1-61477-071-8
First Edition

"A great city is not to be confounded with a populous one."

ARISTOTLE

Over A bridge!
Bellissima Publishing, LLC

Introduction

The name "Budapest" came from combining the names of two cities, "Buda" and "Pest." Originally, there were two separate cities. Today they are connected by eight bridges crossing the Danube. The two cities became one city, a single city, in 1873. According to chronicles of the Middle Ages the name "Buda" came from its founder, Bleda (or Buda) the brother of Attila the Hun. There are several theories about the origin of the name "Pest." One of these theories believes the word "Pest," came from the Roman times, since there was a fortress "Contra-Aquincum" in this region called "Pession." Others think the name "Pest" came from the Slavic word for cave "пещера, peshtera," or from the word for oven "пещ, pesht."

Budapest began as a Celtic settlement that became the Roman capital of Lower Pannonia. Hungarians arrived in the 9th century. Their first settlement was pillaged by the Mongols in 1241-42. The re-established town became one of the centers of Renaissance humanist culture in the 15th century. Following the Battle of Mohács and after nearly 150 years of Ottoman rule, the region entered an age of prosperity in the 18th and 19th centuries. Budapest became a global city after its 1837 unification. It also became the second capital of the Austro-Hungarian Empire, a great power that dissolved in 1918, after World War I. Since that time, there was revolution and more war. Budapest was a part of the USSR until its break-up and the fall of the Berlin Wall.

This book contains a smattering of what you can see and do in Budapest, but not everything. Photographer John D. Weigand and award winning author, attorney and former teacher, Penelope Dyan, traveled there in winter, just before the snow; and were so entranced, they vowed someday to return in the summer and spring. The city of Budapest is considered one of the most beautiful cities in Europe, and there is plenty for a kid to do and see! Dyan and Weigand look at a place through the eyes of a young child to give them a glimpse of what they might see and to let them know, sometimes the world is not such a big place, after all!

Over A Bridge!
Bellissima Publishing, LLC

Over A Bridge!
A Kid's Guide To Budapest, Hungary

Photography By John D. Weigand
Poetry By Penelope Dyan

There are museums, and an opera house (on the Pest side) and Hero's Square! There are fun things to do just everywhere!*

* Budapest has two sides, the Buda side and the Pest side.

There is a Christmas bubble.
And what's more,
in here they collect things
for Hungary's poor.
They have gifts and warm clothes
and some things to eat,
so everyone can have a Christmas treat!
They help Chris Kringle get on his way,
They get everything ready
for Christmas Day!

And you can see art
and paintings everywhere.
There are even paintings
on wall corners
at which you can stare!

There is an artificial ice pond
on which you can skate,
if you are three, four or five,
or even eighty-eight!

A statue of a rider on a horse*
serves the eyes' delight,
with spires and buildings,
framing the site.

*If you walk toward the Hungarian Parliament, you will see the equestrian statue of Ferenc Rákóczi II, the Transylvanian prince who led the revolt against the Habsburgs that turned into the War of Independence. At one time loyal to the Habsburgs, he grew disenchanted with their lack of interest in the Hungarian nobility, and he was imprisoned for conspiring against them, but he escaped to Poland. On the northern lawn, is a statue of Lajos Kossuth for whom the square is named. He was the political leader of the 1848 Hungarian War of Independence from the Habsburgs. Both men fought for the independence of Hungary. Both men were defeated.

And from THIS site
you cannot POSSIBLY hide!
It's a beautiful bridge. . .*
from the park to the other side.

* There are eight bridges that cross the Danube, connecting the two sides of Budapest. This is the Hungarian capital's first bridge, The Chain Bridge, now a monument. This bridge is a fascinating spectacle that attracts many, many tourists to Budapest. The bridge was built at the request of Count István Széchenyi by designer William Tierney Clark and engineer Adam Clark between 1839 and 1849

On the other side of the bridge
you can go right up to the top!
Up, up, and up
until you AT LAST stop!*

* This is the Budapest Castle Hill Funicular, a funicular railway that takes you to the top of the hill on the Buda side of Budapest.

You see some men repairing
the cobblestone street!
And this is something VERY neat.
You stop, and then you watch for awhile.
One of them turns,
and he gives you a smile!

A colorful tiled building of orange
(on the top of the rock)
gives you another reason to pause,
as you walk.

There is a cobblestoned alley,
quite lovely to see.
Beside a building,
out of a sea of cobblestones,
there grows a green tree!

And there are several museums
on THIS Buda side,
and an underground hospital,
where once the injured would hide.
Because, you see, of history here
there is SO much more,
because this place through the ages
was ravaged by war.

The doors of the church are open,
and you can walk inside,
once a mosque, once a castle*
where kings would reside.

* Buda Castle is the historical castle and palace complex of the Hungarian kings in Budapest, first completed in 1265.

The tiled roofs of the church
are works of art,
reminding us of the history
of which THIS place is a part!
You marvel at all the colors and hues,
of the oranges, the grays and the blues,
as here in Buda you can at last,
relive a part of an historical past.
There is the Fisherman's Wall,
a cave and a Roman ruin;
but Mom says, "It's been a long day.
We'll be heading back soon."

You're cold and tired; your feet hurt.
So you stop for warm soup and dessert.
Your mother tells you Marie Antoinette
did not say, "Let them eat cake!"
In 2002, they exposed THAT mistake.
You wonder what it is WAS that Marie Antoinette said,
before she went to the gallows
and then lost her head.
Your mother interrupts your thought.
She says, "Today, you have seen a lot."
You ask what tomorrow has in store.
Your mother replies,
"You'll see some more!"

"This City now doth, like a garment, wear
The beauty of the morning; silent, bare,
Ships, towers, domes, theatres and temples lie
Open unto the fields, and to the sky;
All bright and glittering in the smokeless air."

WILLIAM WORDSWORTH

www.ingramcontent.com/pod-product-compliance
Ingram Content Group UK Ltd.
Pitfield, Milton Keynes, MK11 3LW, UK
UKHW060136240426

12048UKWH00002B/68